Computer Programming

Fundamentals for Absolute Beginners

Alexander Bell

information contained within this document, including, but not limited to, — errors, omissions, or inaccuracies.

Table of Contents

Introduction

Technology is all around us. We are living in a dynamic world where interaction with computers and machines is becoming a reality with each passing day. There was once a time when human basic needs were limited to food, water and shelter. Today, access to the internet is considered a basic need in many parts of the world. If you want to know how true this is, pay attention to the outrage whenever there is a widespread network outage. The outrage is so much it might soon spark a revolution.

Of interest is not just access to the internet, but the applications, tools and resources we connect to. Social media, for example, is driving an industrial revolution of some sort. A lot of activities take place on social networks, and they have nothing to do with basic socialization. Businesses are thriving off the back of social networks. Communities are growing bolder and stronger, participation in activities is heightened and so forth. Yet, this is just one aspect of the internet.

There have been great developments in as far as technology is concerned. Today we are looking forward to a world where artificial intelligence takes center stage. Many research labs and affiliated companies around the world are already experimenting with this. Some companies have already rolled out their prototypes and are making plans for mass production.

With all these developments, where does the average individual come in? What is your place in this highly connected society? Computer programming. Programming is no longer a preserve of a few individuals or geeks who end up in the IT department in some company, typing frantically at their keyboards. Programming is becoming a way of life.

A careful analysis of some of the interactions we have today reveals that for a society that is as heavily leveraged on technology and computers, knowledge of the ins and outs of these systems should be basic, if not compulsory. Some critics fear that in the future, the world might be such a hostile place for individuals who lack basic programming skills.

Developed countries realize this prospect for the future, and have introduced coding camps and training programs for young children. This way, we are nurturing future generations to be tech savvy from the ground-up. Such children learn some basic skills that most people older than them learned at an advanced stage in their lives. If at 9 years old, a child in 2025 has the same knowledge and skills about programming as an 18 year old in 2019, this is progress. This means that the child already has 9 years of experience ahead of their time.

With all the discussions about the future and its prospects regarding programming, it is important to highlight the fact that computer programming is essentially about solving problems in an efficient way. This is the rudimentary reason why we build programs – to solve problems.

Why would a teacher pull out a calculator to get the averages of the class scores in Math when they can key in the data in an Excel sheet and get the averages, totals and all kinds of computations in a second? This is just the simplest iteration of what you can do with basic programming knowledge. You solve problems without going through a longer, resource intensive process.

The beauty of programing is that there is so much to learn. A lot of the things you might have learned in 2010 are no longer relevant in 2019. Some of them were not relevant as early as 2013. This is proof of the fact that technology and associated systems keep changing and they do at a very fast pace. You either keep up, or get left behind.

Programming also opens up so many opportunities to an optimistic individual. There are so many diverse fields where your skills are appreciated. You can carve out a niche for yourself and serve your clients' needs. You will also realize that in as much as there is a lot of development in the world, many companies are still struggling to migrate their operations into a modern and technology-friendly world. Therefore, there are so many opportunities for you to create cutting-edge solutions that such organizations would benefit from.

This book gives you a primer into computer programming. You learn the basics upon which you can lay your foundation. In case you are, like most people, struggling to choose the first programming language you want to study, you will learn that each of these languages is unique to certain developments. Therefore, you can choose where to start depending on what you want to achieve out of your programming career.

As you read on, remember to ease up on the pressure. You cannot learn everything at the same time. If you want to become one of the best in your field, you must be patient, take your time learning, and lay the perfect foundation. Reach out to people around you who can assist whenever you are stuck in a rut. More importantly, simplicity will almost always carry the day.

Chapter 1: Importance of Learning Computer Programming

Programming is one of the most important subjects you can learn today. It is at the forefront in innovation and development of environment friendly solutions to most of the problems we face in the world today. There are several steps involved in developing a program. The role of a programmer is to identify the problem, come up with a feasible solution, write a program to address it, test the program and release the program for the target audience. Once the program is released, the programmer must still keep an eye on it for debugging purposes.

Technology keeps advancing, which means that programming advances in similar fashion. Considering the development environment we have today, you have more than enough reasons to consider a career in computer programming. The following are some reasons why knowledge of computer programming is useful:

Understanding systems

As a programmer, you have intricate knowledge on the performance and features of different programs. Therefore, whenever you interact with any program, you do not just use it as an average user, but your in-depth knowledge allows you to interact with it better than most.

You understand why a given program is necessary and why it does what it does. You also know the limitations of some of the programs you interact with, which means you can come up with feasible expectations of your interaction with the programs so that you can fully utilize the accessories and the equipment available at your disposal.

Educational interaction

One of the fields that has benefited a great deal from programming is the education industry. Programmers are coming up with web applications that can do amazing things. Today people from all walks of life have access to some of the best educational facilities, and from top learning institutions all over the world. All they need to do is get online.

The case for creativity

Programming is a diverse field with lots of experts. Everyone specializes in something, and with specialization comes the need for robust creativity. Mundane techniques barely cut it these days. In an environment where everyone is clamoring to come up with a solution to major problems, creativity is important.

Through programming, you will learn how to do a lot of awesome things, including developing some of the most amazing video games, animations and graphical illustrations. The more creative you are, the easier it is for you to get the attention of powerful entities in the tech industry. Before you know it, you might be head-hunted to work at Google.

Coding for the future

The future is now. Thanks to computer programming, we have a shot at experiencing futuristic concepts today. Developers are currently implementing artificial intelligence in their laboratories. These systems introduce a new way of interacting with computers, computer systems and networks. Together, the future looks bright, especially when you consider the speed with which the Internet of Things (IoT) is advancing.

Programming for the future is not only limited to what happens in development labs worldwide, it is also about the people. Today many countries are reinventing their learning curriculums to make sure that their children are exposed to computer programming at a very early age. This is in realization of the fact that the future is bright with technologically empowered people.

Starting kids on programming at an early age means that they have sufficient time to get used to devices and networks that exist all around them. This also gives them a better chance of changing the way they interact with technology around them. Most of these children will learn the infinite details of how laptops, smartphones and other gadgets work before they get to their teenage years, something that most people in the former generations might have done in their twenties or thirties.

Important life lessons

Computer programming is not just about computers. There are so many other life lessons that you can learn from programming. Considering the interaction diversity you go through from the moment you take a project from conceptualization to implementation, evaluation and maintenance, there are so many lessons to learn in between.

You learn the importance of working with milestones. Milestones help you break down gigantic tasks into smaller, manageable sub-tasks. Completing these tasks makes work easy for you and gives you something to cheer about. In life, celebrating the small wins helps you set the platform for bigger and better things.

You will make a lot of mistakes in programming, especially when you are just starting out. This is not the end of the world. Mistakes are an opportunity for you to learn. Learning from mistakes makes you a better programmer and a better individual in general. It is not just about learning from mistakes, but you also learn that there is no reason to fear failure, or mistakes.

In programming, you will also learn the importance of teamwork. You cannot do it alone. You need a team around you, where everyone pulls their weight. Whenever you see someone receiving accolades for some good project in programming, remember that they never did it alone – most people do not.

These are all important lessons that will define the way you interact with people around you both at work and at home. Some important social connections and networks will be created from these interactions too.

The evolution of technology

A lot of skeptics believe that some years down the line, computers will take over and we will be rendered jobless. Well, most of those who might be rendered jobless are people who cannot adapt. Computers essentially help to make life easier. There are so many systems in use today which have made work easier and more efficient for us. Considering this possibility, knowledge of computer programming will be useful in the near future. While most of the applications and programs are automated, they still need the input of professionals to ensure they work in the right manner. This is only possible when you understand computer programming.

Career path

Whichever career path you choose, it is widely expected that you will need some basic knowledge of programming in the future. Take the marketing industry, for example. It is no longer about printing ads and posting them all over on billboards or coming up with a catchy tune for a radio ad. Marketing has evolved and today, knowledge of analytics, HTML, SQL comes in handy.

Other than that, there is a demand for computer programming experts in the market, but very few people can meet those demands. Technology keeps advancing, and with it the need for experts who understand the technologies in place and more importantly, how to protect and maintain them. This shortage of experienced personnel also means that those who are available earn lucrative salaries.

Chapter 2: Fundamental Programming Concepts

Programming is essentially about solving problems. You write lines of code to save the world. Each program you write must satisfy a specific need, which eventually makes work easier. Before you set out to write a program, you must first understand the issue at hand. Ask yourself what you are trying to solve. One of the best things about using computers is that they are programmed to solve repetitive assignments. Take calculations, for example. You can use your calculator and work out answers to a given series of problems. It might take you a long time, but you will get it done eventually. However, with your computer, all you need is to create a formula and work out all the answers in seconds.

Most problems have more than one possible solution. Some solutions are longer, others are shorter. However, at the end of the day you have an answer. Through programming, you solve problems in the shortest possible way. Programming is about useful resource allocation. You save time solving problems through the programs you write instead of going about them the manual way.

Computer programs are nothing more than a set of instructions that perform a unique instruction when instructed by the computer. There are two different forms of programming, structured programming and object oriented programming.

Structured programming is a model where you run codes in sequence. This model includes control statements that determine the codes that apply in the sequence. Structured programming focuses on improving quality, clarity and the time to development of any computer program.

Object oriented programming on the other hand is a model composed of objects whose data include methods, attributes and procedures. Objects interact independently, sharing messages as opposed to structured programming where there is a strict sequence.

Program structure

All structured programs have the same overall pattern, which includes statements that indicate where the program begins, the variable declaration, and blocks of code that represent the program statements.

In the example below, you see a representation of the fabled *Hello World* in different programming languages. Whichever language you use, the program will print *Hello World* on your screen.

Basic

```
print "Hello World"
```

Perl

```
#!/usr/local/bin/perl – w print "Hello World";
```

Java

```
class helloworld {

        public static void main (String args[]) {

                System.out.println ("Hello World");

        }

    }
```

Oracle PL/SQL

```
CREATE OR REPLACE PROCEDURE helloworld
AS
```

```
BEGIN

    DBMS_OUTPUT.PUT_LINE('Hello World');

END;
```

Pascal
```
program helloworld (output);

begin

    writeln('Hello World');

end.
```

C
```
#include <stdio.h>

void main () {

    printf("Hello World");

}
```

Your program is either poorly structured or well-structured. In a well-structured program, you can see an organized division of components while this is not present in a poorly structured program. Well-structured programs also use appropriate program units and data structures, each of which has a single entry and exit point. Poorly structured programs feature arbitrary flow of control and data structures.

Variable declaration

A variable is a symbolic name that is assigned some information. It is a reference point. The name assigned to a variable represents the information it holds. Information represented by variables is dynamic. As a result the information might change from time to time. However, the operations associated with the variable will not. Variables are storage locations and symbolic names that hold some information or quantity with a value.

Variables are the foundation of all programs and program languages. They help you store information which can be retrieved for use later on. For retrieval, the user simply refers to a word that describes the information.

Say you visit a website and find a small text box that asks for your name. That text box represents a variable. If the developer named the box *clientName*, this would be the symbolic name for the variable.

Therefore, if you write your name in that box, the information you key in is stored in a *clientName* variable. If the developer requests the value that the *clientName* variable holds, the information you typed into that box is displayed.

There are different types of variables, including the following:

- String – refers to a collection of characters.

- Character – unitary character like a punctuation mark or an alphabetic letter.

- Float – also referred to as real. Means to store fractional or real numbers.

- Integer – to store whole numbers or integers.

To use any variable, your computer must identify the data type that is associated with the variable. This is why it is important to declare the type of variables at the very beginning. Declaring variables means you provide the variable data type and a new name. Here's an example (*age, salary* and *middle_initials* are all variables in the C program below):

```
1 | #include <stdio.h>

2 | void main () {

3 | int age;

4 | float salary;

5 | char middle_initial;

6 |age = 28;

7 |salary = 15382409;

8 |middle_initial = "K"

9 |printf ("I am %d years old ", age);

10| printf ("I make %f per year ", salary);

11|printf ("My middle initial is %c ",
                          middle_initial);

}
```

Variables are further grouped into five categories as follows:

NB: The examples below is how it is done in Ruby programming language. The concept is however same for all major programming languages.

- **Constants**

When writing a program, you must declare constants by capitalizing the first letters in the name of the variable. Constants store data that you might not need to change. By default, most programming languages other than Ruby do not permit value changes to constants. However, just because Ruby allows you to change constant variables does not mean that you should.

This is what a constant variable looks like:

```
1 | MY_CONSTANT = 'I am reachable throughout the
process.'
```

- **Global variables**

Global variables are indicated with a dollar sign at the beginning of the variable name. They override all the boundaries and are applicable all through the app.

This is what a global variable looks like:

```
1 | $var = 'I am also reachable throughout the
process.'
```

- **Class variables**

Class variables must be declared with two @ signs at the beginning of the variable. They are used by different instances of a class.

This is what a class variable looks like:

```
1 | @@instances = 3
```

- **Instance variables**

Instance variables are declared with one @ sign. They are useful in object oriented programming.

This is what an instance variable looks like:

```
1 | @var = 'I am available throughout the current
process.'
```

- **Local variables**

Of all variables you come across in programming, local variables are among the most frequently used. They conform to all boundary scopes. When declaring a local variable, you do not use either @ or $, neither do you need to capitalize the variable name.

This is what a local variable looks like:

```
1 | var = 'Pass me around to scope boundaries.'
```

Looping structures

Remember when we mentioned earlier that computers allow you to perform calculations repeatedly? This is what happens with loop structures. Loop structures enable you to repeatedly run lines of code, even if it is one line of code. The idea here is to replicate the statement within a loop structure until you meet a given condition, whether *True* or *False.*

If the code does not have a functioning exit routine, it is referred to as an infinite loop. This looping structure will persist until it is detected by the operating system and terminated. When terminated in such a manner, you receive an error. It can also terminate as a result of another event occurring, like scheduling the program to terminate after a predetermined amount of time.

Control structures

Control structures refer to programming blocks that analyze variables and determine the best direction to proceed according to the parameters provided. From basic understanding, control structures are the decision-makers in computer programming. They determine how the computer should respond when specific parameters and conditions are upheld.

Whenever you run a program, your computer reads all the code in the same way you read a book. This is what is referred to as code flow. In the course of reading all the code, your computer might encounter a scenario where it needs to skip from one point to another, or repeat a specific part of the code to perform some activity. There are strict rules that make this possible. These rules necessitate a specific decision which affects the way code flows. The specific decision is referred to as a control structure.

Syntax

Syntax refers to the set or rules that guide the combination of symbols which are structured in a specific programming language. If you try to access a document that has the wrong syntax, you end up with a syntax error. Syntax in programming, therefore, works the same way spelling and grammar does in linguistic classes.

An English statement with poor spelling and lots of grammar mistakes is difficult, if not impossible to understand. This is the same thing that happens with syntax errors. Since your computer cannot understand the code, it cannot execute it, hence a syntax error.

Things are, however, more complicated with computers. In English, you can understand what the sentence means, especially if it has simple errors. In computer programming, the tiniest syntax error in your code will render it useless and unreadable. This is why programmers are often encouraged to focus not only on logic when writing programs, but on syntax too.

Computer programming syntax is further classified into the following:

- Words – lexical content that represent how tokens are formed from characters.

- Phrases – grammatical content that represent how phrases are formed from tokens.

Context – determinants that indicate among other things, whether types are valid, the variables that names refer to and so forth.

Chapter 3: Algorithms in Programming

While variables are the data stores in programming, algorithms are the building blocks. It is through algorithms that the software you use can fetch the data you need. Algorithms are the bridge between normal language and computer language. Your challenges are translated into the unique language running your software, before it is translated back to a language you can understand and interpret.

The easiest way to conceptualize an algorithm is a cooking recipe. Recipes outline every step of the way from food preparation to the point the meal is ready to serve. This is what algorithms do. They outline the necessary steps your computer must follow to achieve your intended goals.

While still on the recipe example, in programming we would refer to recipes as **procedures**, ingredients as **inputs** and the final outcome of your recipe as an **output**. Algorithms describe how to perform a task, and each time that algorithm is executed, your computer will perform it in the same manner.

To prevent confusion, we must mention that algorithms are not computer code. Algorithms are written in plain language that you understand. It could be English, Korean, Chinese, you name it. Algorithms are precise and have three sections: the start, the middle and the end. When writing an algorithm, you will actually indicate *start* for the first step, and *end* for the last step.

Algorithms must only include the necessary information to complete a task. They must be precise so that they lead you to an efficient solution. When writing algorithms, it is wise to number your steps, though it is not mandatory. Some programmers use pseudocode, a semi-programming language that explains the steps followed in an algorithm.

Here is an example of an algorithm that requests user email addresses:

Step 1: Start

Step 2: Create variable to receive user email address

Step 3: Clear variable if not empty

Step 4: Request user email address

Step 5: Store response in variable

Step 6: Verify if email address is valid

Step 7: Invalid address? Back to Step 3

Step 8: End

Here is an example of an algorithm that adds two numbers:

Step 1: Start

Step 2: Declare variables num3, num4 and sum.

Step 3: Read variables num3 and num4.

Step 4: Add num3 to num4 and assign result to sum.

$$sum \leftarrow num3+num4$$

Step 5: Display sum

Step 6: End

Here is an algorithm that determines the largest of three values:

Step 1: Start

Step 2: Declare variables x, y and z.

Step 3: Read variables x, y and z.

Step 4: If x>y

If x>z

Display x is the largest number.

Else

Display z is the largest number.

Else

If y>z

Display y is the largest number.

Else

Display z is the largest number.

Step 5: End

This is how simple algorithms are. They state what you need in the procedure. A good algorithm must have the following features:

- Clear and precise definition of the input and output

- All steps must be simple and clear.

- The chosen algorithm should be the most effective way to arrive at a solution.

- There should be no computer code in an algorithm.

There are several classes of algorithms and data structures that you need to learn about in programming. You will use them almost everywhere in developmental and competitive programming. Here are the main algorithms:

Sort algorithms

This is one of the largest categories of algorithms that you will learn in programming. These algorithms allow you to arrange a list in a desired order. Each programming language today comes with its own sorting library. However, it is still important to learn about these:

- Merge sort

- Counting sort

- Heap sort

- Bucket sort

- Quick sort

Knowledge of these algorithms is not enough. What is more important is knowing how, where and when they are necessary.

Search algorithms

There are two popular types of search algorithms: breadth-first search as used in group data structures, and binary search used in linear data structures. Binary searches are recommended when you need an efficient search on a dataset that is sorted. The concept here is to continually halve the dataset until you narrow your options down to a solitary item. A common use of this algorithm is when you search for the name of a film in an assorted list of movies. The algorithm conducts a binary search by string matching to deliver the right result.

The search algorithm comes in handy in your map when you need to find the shortest possible route from one point to the other, especially if you have many options. It is also used to create intelligent bots in AI. Search engines are some of the biggest users of search algorithms, by trawling the internet for appropriate results before they are displayed.

String matching and parsing

One of the biggest problems you will solve in your life as a software programmer is pattern searching and matching. To do this, you need proper knowledge of the following:

- String matching (KMP algorithm)

The Knuth-Morris-Pratt (KMP) algorithm is applicable in instances where you need to match short patterns in long strings. One common example is executing a *Ctrl+F* command for a keyword. Basically what you are doing is pattern matching the keyword pattern all through the document.

- String parsing (Regular expression)

You will also learn to parse over predefined restrictions to validate strings in development, especially for parsing and matching URLs in web development.

Hashing algorithms

Hash algorithms are some of the most popular algorithms used today, especially when looking for a specific ID or key in reference to some dataset. Data retrieved through hashing algorithms is identified by its unique index. Before hashing algorithms were available, such searches were conducted through a combination of binary and sorting search algorithms.

Hashing algorithms help you search a list of items to determine whether a specific value is already present within. Routers also use this algorithm to identify and store IP addresses of devices connected to it. This way, no two devices can be assigned the same IP address on the network.

Dynamic programming

Dynamic programming algorithms help you solve problems by breaking down the complex concerns into smaller discernable units. Once this is done, each small unit is solved independent of the others, and the solutions stored to memory. Once all the small units are solved, the solutions help you work your way up to the ultimate solution to the complex problem that necessitated the algorithm.

Think about it this way, when you write down 2+2+2+2+2, you know the answer is 10. If you add another +2 at the end, you immediately calculate that the answer is 12. You arrive at 12 so fast because in your memory you already know the answer to the first set, so you only need to add one set of 2. This is how a dynamic programming algorithm works.

Primality testing algorithms

In order to figure out whether some random number is a prime number or not, you can use probabilities or deterministic methods. This algorithm is commonly used in cryptography, especially in encryption and decryption. They are also used in hash tables as hash functions.

Exponentiation by squaring

Try calculating 2^{32}. By default, you must perform 32 calculations involving the number 2. This is too much work. However, through this algorithm, you only need to do this 5 times. This algorithm is also referred to as binary exponentiation.

In binary exponentiation, you can compute large positive integer powers very fast in the format $O(log_2N)$. The example we have provided is one of the simplest. Binary exponentiation can also be used to compute square matrices and polynomial powers.

Chapter 4: Data Structures

Data structures refer to data elements that provide the best possible method of data organization and storage in computer systems, so that it can be retrieved and used efficiently. There are several examples of data structures, such as stacks, linked lists, arrays and queues. In computer programming, you will use data structures in virtually all fields, from graphics to artificial intelligence and compiler design.

You should master knowledge of data structures because they form the foundation of algorithms used in computer science. If you understand data structures, it is easier for you to manage all data you have access to in the most efficient manner. Since data structures help in data storage and retrieval, they help to improve the performance of any programs and software you are running.

Any application or program you write will have data structures as its backbone. One of the most difficult experiences you will have is choosing the right structure for the program you write. The following are some of the important terms you will come across in data structures:

- **Data** – Data refers to a collection of values in the data structures. For example, patient names and phone records are data about the patients.

- **Field** – Field refers to a unit of information that represents an attribute of a given entity.

- **Entity and attributes** – An entity refers to a class of specific objects in a data structure. Each entity has unique attributes, which refers to a unique property that makes the entity stand out.

- **File** – A file refers to a group of records collected from one entity. Take the example of 50 patients in a hospital wing. There might be 30 records in a specific file where each record has data about each of the patients.

- **Record** – A record is a collection of different data items. Using the example of patients in a hospital, information like their names, phone information, and previous hospital visits can be compiled to form records of the patients.

- **Group items** – Group items refer to pieces of data that are subordinate to a specific data set. In patient name, for example, you can have the first name, middle name and last name as group items.

Why do we need data structures? With time, programmers are facing the challenge of solving problems that are more complex than before. As a result, the complexity of data being handled is also growing. Other than the complexity, the amount of data handled is also increasing. With these advances, some challenges arise which might affect the efficiency of programs written, and if unchecked, they can compromise the integrity of the respective programs. These are some of the problems arising:

Multiple requests

Picture a situation where thousands, if not millions, of users are trying to retrieve some information from a web server at the same time. In such a scenario, it is highly likely that the server will buckle under the weight of these requests.

To mitigate against this risk, data structures come in handy. The data is organized in a manner such that only the data items that are needed are searched, instead of running the queries through all the data.

Data searches

Think about managing a hospital that hosts thousands of patients each day. If you need to search for something, the application must search through thousands of records. Without the right parameters, say searching for data through an entire month, the process takes longer and will slow down the machine, too.

Processing speed

You need a high processing speed to handle a large amount of data. The processing speed you have built into the program will not suffice over time. You will need to upgrade as your needs increase. Without this, the present processor might struggle to process the necessary data with the same efficiency it had earlier on.

While addressing these three challenges, we realize that data structures are important for several reasons. First, data structures introduce efficiency in data handling. When data is organized in ordered arrays, hash tables, binary search trees and so forth, data searches are easier and not resource-intensive.

Second, data structures are resilient and can be reused. Once you implement the desired data structure and have proof that it works, you can copy the same in another instance where it will work just as well. You therefore do not need to spend time constructing a new data structure.

Finally, data structures introduce the concept of abstraction. This means that when a client requests data from the front end of the application, they have access to the interface. They do not have access to the back end where all the implementation takes place. This also protects vital information from falling into the wrong hands.

Classification of data structures

Linear data structures

If all the elements in a data structure are arranged in a linear pattern, it is a linear data structure. All the elements in this structure are ordered in a non-hierarchical manner. While every other element in this structure has a predecessor and successor, the first and last element in the structure do not. Some examples include:

- **Linked lists**

Linked lists are linear data structures that keep a list within the memory. They can also be viewed as a group of nodes, each pointing to an adjacent node.

- **Arrays**

Arrays are a group of similar data sets. Each of the data items are referred to as array elements. Elements of an array have similar variable names but each of the elements has a unique subscript (index number), as shown: student[1], student[2], student[3].....student[56], student[57]

- **Stacks**

Stacks refer to a linear list where you can only insert or delete content at one end, the top. Stacks are abstract data types, and for this reason you can use them in most programming languages.

- **Queue**

Queue refers to a linear list where elements can only be added at the rear end, and deleted only from the front end. Like stacks, queues are abstract data structures. Since queues are opened at both ends, they employ the first-in-first-out principle when sorting data.

Non-linear data structures

These are data structures that do not follow any sequence. Every item in this structure is connected to one or more elements or items, all which do not follow any sequence either. Some examples are:

- **Graphs**

These are graphic illustrations of different elements in a data structure in the form of edges and vertices. While graphs and trees can serve the same purpose, graphs have cycles while trees cannot.

- **Trees**

These are multi-level data structures whose elements follow a predetermined hierarchy relationship, referred to as nodes. Leaf nodes are found at the bottom of the hierarchy, while root nodes are at the top. At the end of each node, you find pointers that point to other nodes close by.

Data in trees is often used to indicate a parent-child relationship between the associated nodes. Other than the leaf nodes, all the others can represent multiple children. On the same note, all nodes can belong to one parent apart from the root node.

Data structure operations

Having seen the components of data structures, let's look at some of the operations that are permitted on them:

- **Traverse**

Data structures hold lots of data elements. Traversing refers to the action of visiting each element to perform a given operation.

- **Insert**

Insert refers to the process of adding new elements to a data structure irrespective of the location where the action takes place. Take note that the following rule applies to insertion:

For data structure of size **n**, you can only insert a maximum of **n-1** elements.

- **Delete**

Delete refers to removing one or more elements from the data structure. This action can be performed at any point in the data structure.

- **Search**

Search refers to finding the exact location of an element in the data structure. This is done through binary search or linear search algorithms.

- **Sort**

Sort refers to the action of organizing elements in the data structure in a predetermined order. This can be done through a number of algorithms, including bubble sort, selection sort and insertion sort.

- **Merge**

Merging refers to the process of joining two lists, **List X** and **List Y** of sizes **A** and **B**. The two lists must share similar elements. After merging, you end up with **List Z** of size **(A+B)**.

Chapter 5: Programming Languages

What we refer to as programming languages are simply grammatical rules that instruct a computing device or a computer on how to perform a given assignment. Programming languages are used in web development and include web clients, web content and server scripting, alongside the network's security. There are hundreds of programming languages today, each of which features a unique keyword pattern, and syntax used to organize the instructions.

Whenever we mention programming languages, in essence we are referring to high-level programming languages. High-level programming languages are relatively simple compared to normal human languages. However, they are complex when pitted against machine languages, which is the language computers understand. In programming, you will learn that every computer has a unique machine language that it responds to.

The mention of programming languages, however, often refers to high-level languages like Pascal and C which allow programmers to code programs which are independent of the computer they write it on. These languages are often considered high-level because of their likeness to human languages, compared to machine languages.

Assembly languages act as the link between high-level languages and machine languages. While assembly languages are almost similar to machine languages, they stand out because programming them is easier. When writing an assembly language, you can swap numbers for names. In machine languages, however, you only use numbers.

Fourth generation languages (4GL) are a level above high-level languages. They are a representation of computer languages that are very close to human languages, and furthest from machine languages.

The hierarchy of computer languages is, therefore, as follows:

1st Generation – Machine language (1GL)

This generation is at times referred to as low-level programming because they are used to program computers at the machine level, which is one of the lowest abstraction levels. It is also the native computer system language, and it is written in binary numbers only. Machine language has the following advantages:

- Programs written in machine language are efficient and can be executed faster by the computers.

- No resource cost of translation, because the computers execute the languages directly.

- Efficient memory consumption since all data bits can be tracked.

2nd Generation – Assembly language (2GL)

Assembly language is also one of the low-level programming languages. In this language, mnemonics are introduced when writing programs in reference to operands and opcodes in the instructions.

Programs written in assembly languages are less susceptible to errors, and as a result they are easier to maintain. Programmers also find it easier to understand and edit assembly language programs compared to machine language programs.

3rd Generation – High-level programming language (3GL)

While machine and assembly languages are straightforward and easy to comprehend, they still posed some challenges. High-level programming languages were introduced to bridge the gap and eliminate some of the challenges programmers experienced with the earlier languages.

3GL are considered high-level because they allow you to focus on the logical element of the programs you write, without worrying about the computer system's intricate architecture. As a result, programmers find it easier to learn, develop and understand a program.

Programs written in 3GL are not susceptible to as many errors as the earlier generations. They are also easier to maintain. Programmers can also write these programs in a shorter time compared to the earlier generations. Some of the best examples of 3GL include C, C++, Fortran and Algol.

One of the greatest achievements of 3GL is allowing independence in the use of language architecture. What this means is that you are no longer restricted to using a given environment or processor, which would require the use of a compiler to write code for a computer system. In the case of Java, for example, you have intermediate code operated by a virtual machine. This offers even more architectural independence to programmers.

3GL is heavily hinged on structured programming, with languages like C. However, advancements later on introduced functional and object-oriented programming, which is one of the most important fields in programming today, with languages like Python, Java, C#, Delphi and C++.

4th Generation – Very high-level languages (4GL)

Very high-level languages were introduced to help in mitigating the cost, effort and time programmers need to build software applications. These languages help the programmer become more efficient. The focus is on improving the productivity of the programmer.

4GL languages allow programmers to implement databases, which help in efficient data management. Building on this, the programmer can spend a shorter time, less effort and spend less to build applications compared to the earlier generation languages. Programs that are built using very high-level languages are also easily portable. Some examples include ColdFusion, CSS, SOL, SPSS, SAS, Oracle Forms, and SQL.

4GL languages introduce statement power and higher abstraction to improve on the 3GL languages. As a result these languages allow the programmer enhanced development speed and fewer errors, by simply reducing the effort the programmer needs to invest in writing programs.

4GL applications are built to serve a specific purpose. As a result, they have a very high potential for solving problems. However, they are not always efficient, and when problems arise, you might end up with unmaintainable or inelegant code. While 3GL focuses on software engineering, 4GL focuses on systems engineering and problem solution.

5th Generation – Neural networks and artificial intelligence (5GL)

In this generation, the emphasis is on constraint programming. 5GL languages are primarily used in building artificial neural networks and artificial intelligence. This is the future, at least at this point in time.

5GL languages can query databases faster than the predecessors, which makes them highly efficient in a fast-paced world. Other than that, users also have the advantage of communicating with the computer systems efficiently through simple user commands. Basically, users will soon speak to computer systems in the same manner they do to their peers. Some examples are OPS5, Prolog and Mercury.

5GL languages improve on the work done in the previous generations by overriding the need for algorithms, and instead focusing on constraints. They solve problems without the input of the programmer, which is a stark difference from 4GL languages which build unique applications to solve problems.

As a result, the role of a programmer using 5GL languages is to ensure the prerequisite conditions are met for problems to be solved, instead of thinking about how to implement algorithms or routines to solve the problems.

Characteristics of programming languages

When choosing the best programming language for you to build applications and solutions, you need to make sure the program is consistent in terms of semantics and syntax. The program must also have the right tools necessary for testing, development, debugging, and maintenance. The following are some of the important things you should consider when choosing a reliable programming language:

- **Simplicity**

Each programming language is unique. Some of them share a few features. You need a language that is easy to understand and work with. Simplicity is one of the most important things in programming. If the program is easy to understand, it will be easier for you to use.

The language should also have simple, clear and unified concepts that are easy to understand. The simpler the language, the easier it is to read programs written in it. This also means they are easier to maintain.

- **Compact**

Programmers need languages that allow them to express their intended operations efficiently. A compact program allows you to do this without writing too much code. Any language that is too verbose is often frowned upon by programmers.

- **Efficiency**

A good language should allow easy translation into machine language, and execute smoothly. Apart from that, they should not be resource intensive on the memory. To enable this, the language must have a comprehensive language translator that balances time and space allocation needs accordingly.

- **Abstraction**

Abstraction refers to the process of using complex operations and structures in such a manner that you can ignore most of the details. The level of abstraction affects the writability of a programming language. Object-oriented programming, for example, has a very high level of abstraction. As a result, it is easier to write programs in.

- **Natural**

The best program is always one that is naturally suited for the area in which it is applied. This means it should have the data structures, operators, syntax and control structures to enable programmers write programs efficiently.

- **Structured**

A structured language is one whose features enable programmers to write programs according to structured programming concepts. With this in mind, programmers can address problems from a logical perspective and, in the process, having to deal with fewer errors when writing programs to solve problems.

Chapter 6: Web Programming

Web programming, also referred to as web development, is an elaborate process where programmers build dynamic applications for use on the internet. Some of the popular web applications today include business platforms like Amazon and social networks like Facebook and Twitter.

While these are some of the top names in the industry, it is easy to assume that web programming is hard. It takes a lot of practice, but in essence web development is one of the easiest forms of coding you can learn as a programmer. When writing code for a website, you see immediate results, which help you determine whether you are doing the right thing, or need to ask for help. Besides, today there are so many tools and resources available online that you can use to learn.

There are two categories of web development; front-end development and back-end development. Front-end development is also known as client-side development. It involves building the side of the application that the user interacts with whenever they load the application. This includes the design and content, and how the user interacts with the application. Front-end development is primarily written in JavaScript, CSS and HTML.

Back-end development, also referred to as server-side development deals with everything else that takes place behind the scenes. Users do not see this, but it is the engine that powers what they interact with whenever they are online. You need a database for the back-end, which will eventually power the front-end. There are many programming languages that can be used to build the server-side, including Java,

Python, PHP, and Perl.

Factors to consider when choosing a programming language

Given that there are so many languages available, it might not be easy for you to choose one for your project. There are some factors, however, that can guide your choice, and help make your work easier, as follows:

- **Tool support**

You should always consider working with a programming language that has all the tools you need to build your project effortlessly. This way, you will not just manage to build the application, but you can also maintain it without a hitch.

- **Size of the project**

The sheer size of some projects necessitates the use of specific languages. Some languages might be effective, but their performance is inhibited when the project scales up in size. A lot of startup companies realize this some years down the line. Once the business needs and application resource consumption grows, they have to switch to a different language.

- **Library support**

Before you settle on a given language, make sure you consider the library constraints. Ensure that the library available will not just meet your needs, but will also solve other needs arising down the line.

- **Elasticity**

Flexibility is one of the key features you must look at. For your projects, ensure you use a language that allows you to scale the application accordingly over time. This means you should manage to add or remove some features and programs into the application without affecting the performance.

- **Platform choice**

Always think about the platform upon which the application will run. While most languages support different platforms, their suitability might not be pleasant across the board. Take programs written in C, for example. These programs are best suited for Linux and Windows-based systems. While you might experiment with other platforms, the performance might not be as you would experience in a Windows or Linux environment.

Programming languages

If you are a beginner in web programming or software development, you might have come across so many languages to the point where you are unsure where to start. A lot of people have been there. There are so many languages to choose from. However, you need to know where to begin, and how to build on what you have learned. Here are some of the top programming languages in use today.

Python

Python stands out today as one of the most versatile programming languages in the world. When using Python, you can write code and at the same time run it without using a compiler. Python further boasts support for code readability.

41

What this means is that its syntax structure allows you to write a few lines of code to make a point. This is also possible in C++ and Java. The interesting thing about Python is that while it is an advanced language, it is very easy, and beginner programmers can pick up on it very fast.

There are so many popular applications currently running on Python, including Google, Yahoo, Pinterest and Instagram. Most of these are websites and applications that are heavy on memory usage, which means that Python is not just perfect for automated memory management, it also features a very big library and supports various paradigms in development.

CSS

Cascading Style Sheets, CSS, is a markup language. It defines the way a website or web page appears, when coupled with HTML. Some of the elements that make up CSS determine things like the font style and size, colors and any other design features of the website.

CSS helps developers create visually pleasing websites. It has also come in handy in the development of appealing mobile applications too. CSS features a language syntax that is almost similar to XHTML and HTML. As a result, the language syntaxes can work together without a hitch.

Java

Java is one of the most in-demand languages today. It is widely used in developing mobile apps and games. It is object-oriented, and is favored by most developers because it can be used across different platforms. Therefore, a program written on a Windows-based machine can still run on a Mac OS device.

JavaScript

JavaScript is currently one of the best programing languages you need to learn. It empowers you to manage the browser, allow front-end scripts to run, edit and display content on the website and so forth. JavaScript allows for asynchronous interaction between users and the application.

JavaScript is one of the most popular languages given its prevalence in game development and building desktop applications. All the major browsers support JavaScript, so you do not need plug-ins or a compiler to run an application.

JavaScript is a functional language. Objects in JavaScript are first-class, associating with their characteristics and functions. An example is a nested function, which is a function inside a function.

This is also one of the most dynamic languages because types are related to values, not variables. As a result, you can test project types in several ways. JavaScript is an object-oriented language, and as such all the objects within its environment are associative arrays.

PHP

Hypertext Processor, PHP, is a server-side language which is recommended for use in web development and other regular programming needs. PHP has been around since 2004, but currently powers hundreds of millions of websites all over the world.

Given that PHP is an interpreted script language, it is ideal for back-end programming because of the need for an interpreter. It is suitable for this type of programming because you can run server services in the background while still developing the application or website.

Ruby

Ruby is a dynamic programming language that has been around since 1993. Ruby is ideal for building websites and mobile applications. As a highly scalable language, it provides an astute balance between functional programming and imperative programming.

Ruby is not just easy to understand, it is also one of the easiest languages to write. However, for beginner developers who are just getting into Ruby, it is wise to start with Ruby on Rails. Ruby on Rails makes it easier for you to work with Ruby, and enjoy the experience.

Ruby is often recommended for websites or web servers that encounter lots of traffic. Some popular examples include Twitter and Hulu.

Swift

Swift is another general-purpose, compiled, open-source language owned by Apple Inc. Programmers who are interested in building apps native to the Mac OS and iOS platforms will find it quite useful.

If you have experience with Ruby and Python, you will find Swift relatively easy to use. It was specifically designed to be beginner-friendly, and is a better, faster, more secure and easier language to comprehend and debug compared to

Objective C, its predecessor.

Swift uses less code compared to Objective C, and the syntax almost resembles normal English. Therefore, it is one of the easiest languages to write for programmers who have experience with C++, C#, Python, Java, and JavaScript.

One of the challenges you might experience when programming in Swift is that there are not so many programmers who use it, especially when you compare with other open-source languages.

SQL

Structured Query Language, commonly identified in its abbreviated form SQL is a programming language that was specifically written for database operations. Data manipulation, storage and retrieval are some of the key features in SQL. A lot of web based frameworks run SQL today, given that it is effective in maintaining database integrity, is secure and maintains data precision.

Objective C

This is an object-oriented programming language native to Apple Inc. and built for iOS and OS X APIs (application programming interfaces) and operating systems. It is also a general purpose language, and is often referred to as Hybrid C, given that it adds some features to C.

C

C is similar to C++. It is a general purpose language that is often used to build supporting elements for other languages like Java, C++ and Python. This means that most of the supported languages borrow some features from C, such as standard libraries, syntax and control structures. This explains why it is always advisable that you learn C++ and C before you expand your knowledge to other languages, so that you have a firm foundation in the basics.

C-Sharp (C#)

Microsoft developed C# in 2000 as an object-oriented programming language. It is popular in desktop applications, and became an integral part of applications built for Windows 8 and Windows 10. To run C# therefore, you must have the .NET framework installed on your computer. C# was built to compete with Java.

Compared with C++, C# has logical and consistent code, which is one of the reasons why it is one of the best languages for beginners to grasp. C# is a statically typed language, which means that you can check your code before you run it into applications. Therefore, it is easier to identify errors when programming in C#.

C++

C++ is a case-sensitive programming language. It is general purpose, and presents programmers with the necessary tools for memory manipulation at a low level. C++ is an interesting language because it combines the features of high-level languages and low-level languages. As a result, it is often construed as a mid-level language.

Primarily, C++ is an object-oriented language, thanks to the following inherent features:

- Data hiding

- Inheritance

- Encapsulation

- Polymorphism

C++ is a superset of C, so they share a lot of similarities. This also means that if you write a program in C, it is also a C++ program. C++ is a very detailed language. For beginners, it is advisable that you focus on the concepts instead of the details, lest you get confused.

So, where does this leave you? The best place for you to start depends on what you want to pursue in your career. If you feel database management is right for you, you should start with C++ or C to become an SQL developer.

Back-end developers will find JavaScript, PHP, Python, C#, Ruby and Python handy, while front-end developers should be okay with JavaScript.

If you plan to delve into game development, focus on C# and C++. Mobile app developers should emphasize Java, Swift and C#. Programmers who are interested in building desktop applications should focus on Python, C++ and Java.

Remember that this is one of the most dynamic industries. Therefore, expect new releases and updates from time to time. It is difficult to advise anyone which programming language is best because choices depend on needs assessment.

Chapter 7: Security in Programming

Financially motivated crime is one of the common reasons why hackers come after systems, applications and programs. Breaches happen all the time. Some entities do not report when they should. As long as your program is connected to the internet, you will always be at risk of attack. Sadly, there is not much you can do to prevent someone from trying to attack your system. What you can do is make things a bit difficult for them.

Most of the vulnerabilities that are exploited by hackers are often in the application layer of the programs. Therefore, this is one place you should consider focusing on whenever you are writing a program. What can you do to protect your networks and systems as a programmer?

Design security

Many hackers today use bugs to exploit weaknesses in networks and systems, allowing them privileges to destroy, alter or steal data. Cross-site scripting and SQL injections are some of the popular techniques hackers use. The sad bit is that these are techniques that are very easy to circumvent, but somehow, they still manage to run amok in the system.

One of the strategies you can consider is securing your design from the ground up. As you are building apps and writing code, ensure security is one of your key considerations. It is easier to build an app that is protected than build an insecure app and work on security later on.

When security is part of the development concept, your security concerns are reduced. Ensure all the necessary security policies are considered and applied in your development architecture. Analyze all the code you are using to detect any flaws and address them as soon as possible.

Simplicity

You do not need to pull tricks out of your sleeves to protect your development environment. Complex attempts at security will often fail. In fact, when you attempt a very complicated process, you will easily mess up, leaving yourself exposed in more ways than you know.

A simple approach will always work best. A simple approach means that you are aware of what you are doing, and how it is supposed to work. If something goes awry, you will not miss it. However, if you implement several processes and tools to protect your services, chances are high that you will not follow all the applicable rules as they should be followed, which means you will be unable to protect your development environment.

It is always advisable to work with a security apparatus that you already understand and trust and build on it gradually, instead of introducing a new and unrelated security apparatus.

Embrace secure coding

Secure coding is a set of guidelines that make sure you write programs that are protected from flaws. Today, secure coding is one of the most important things any developer must embrace. You need to learn about different tools and techniques to help you with this. Running insecure programs leaves you at risk of countless challenges, including compromised data, denial of service attacks, service loss, financial suits and so forth.

In the development stage, it is advisable that you think about security like a hacker. A hacker is essentially a professional coder, an expert to be precise. Their motives might not always be negative. Some hackers just lurk around the ecosystem trying to study what you do and then leave. Others interfere with your operations. Whichever the case, anyone who has no business or privilege accessing your systems should not be there in the first place.

Every hacker has a different motive. As you write your programs, think about these motives, and how they might pose challenges to your program. If you can do this, you will also think about possible ways of preventing the possible risks from occurring. It is better to be safe than sorry.

Everyone is at risk

Never assume that your program is the most secure program around. There are so many risks out there today. You can be attacked in ways you never imagined. Some attackers might also piggyback on other players to gain access to your system.

When you believe you are always at risk, you will take the necessary precautions to ensure you are not vulnerable. Securing your programs is a round-the-clock task. Talk to experts in your industry about security so you know how to stay safe. Consult your peers, especially those who are experienced in such matters, so they can advise you on what to do and how to go about protecting your program and network. If you make security a common concern and a community effort, you stand a better chance than going it all alone.

Security by obscurity

Time and again programmers are advised that security by obscurity is not one of the best ways to ensure systems are protected. This is one of the easiest ways to fail at protecting your networks, and a lot of companies have failed miserably.

One of the common methods of security by obscurity is to insist that users create very strong passwords. It is unwise to rely on this alone. Today hackers have so many ways of bypassing such techniques.

What you need to do is ensure you have mechanisms in place to identify and analyze inconsistencies in the data you handle, protect your database and more importantly, ensure all inputs into your system are sanitized. The best way to protect your system is always to assume the system is already compromised. In this case, you will always be working round the clock to seek out damages and fix them. You will also work hard to implement proper testing mechanisms.

Privileged access

Make sure your applications can only be accessed by users or accounts with the correct privileges. When assigning privileges to accounts, think about the users and their immediate responsibilities. Only allow access where necessary. This should also apply for applications and passwords.

Think about those applications which offer default passwords to first-time users. To prevent unnecessary risks, make sure the default password sent to such users is not the same. The passwords should also be used within a limited timeframe. Always encourage users to change their passwords as soon as they receive the default password.

Chapter 8: The Future of Programming

People often say two things are certain in this life, taxes and death. Well, technological advancement is the third. Set aside some time today and talk to the older folks around you, like your grandparents, and tell them about your work as a coder. Try to explain to them what you do and why it is important. Chances are that they will not understand, and probably feel you are playing a trick on them.

How many people are frowned upon by people around them because they seem to be sitting in front of their computer screens all day? Everyone else who does not understand what computer programming is about will never get what you do. Some people even blatantly ask you how you make money from that computer. They are used to the conventional ways of toiling hard and getting paid, oblivious of the fact that the world is changing.

Today we talk about cryptocurrency, one of the latest in a list of disruptive technologies that has shaken the traditional industries. While cryptocurrencies were introduced as alternative currencies that aim to do away with the challenges facing the traditional fiscal currencies, they have morphed into something else. Some of the cryptocurrencies are in essence budding development environments where programmers build some amazing projects.

Coding is a way of teaching the computer to do something by writing a special language that it can understand. Code that was written in the 1990s is very different from code that is in use today. Over the past few years, we have witnessed the birth of so many amazing programs, and the fall of many others.

Some companies are dying a slow death, and we will witness it all. Take Yahoo, for example. A few years back, it was unfathomable to think that Yahoo would one day be struggling to stay relevant. There was a time when Yahoo was the go-to platform for anyone who needed an email address. This is not the case today. In fact, millennials frown upon Yahoo. If you still own a Yahoo email address, someone would openly wonder why you still do.

One thing that we can be sure about the future of computer programming is that it is not static for anything or anyone. You must be dynamic and espouse a willingness to adapt just as much as the industry grows. The following are some things we can look forward to in the coming years:

Abstract programming

Developers can look forward to a future of increased abstraction. What this means is that you will soon interact with technologies without the need for containers or servers. Low-level coding will be a thing of the past. This is something that many programmers are already experiencing.

All these changes are informed by the need to move away from infrastructure-based computing. Infrastructure is a waste of time. Tech giants are already moving to the next frontier and embracing cloud computing. This also brings to the fore the issue of offering as-a-service models (XaaS).

Microsoft is one of the companies that is already exploring this and has started implementing it on a wide scale. We see many business-as-a-service (BaaS) models, software-as-a-service (SaaS) and so forth. The emphasis is not on building the physical products, but on how native applications can be built to run as services.

On the same note, environment independence will be a thing of the past. The years when Microsoft would develop applications that would only work on Windows products and not iOS, OS X, Linux and so forth, are long gone. Today a lot of developers are working towards cross-platform applications. This unity means that once a program or application is rolled out, the dev team only has to work on offering it as a subscription-based service, instead of spending time building another app for a different platform.

Artificial intelligence (AI)

There have been many arguments about AI in the past. Some people worry that AI will replace developers. There is no need to fear AI. In fact, we are moving into a future where developers will need to have AI in their toolkit. With most of the world gearing towards AI, it would be a pity to be left behind.

Think about it, Microsoft already introduced an update into one of the latest Windows 10 updates which allows developers to experiment with machine learning models. These technologies are a reflection of the prospects for the future. They, however, are not going to replace programmers. You are still an important part of the development environment.

Universal programming language

This might sound far-fetched, but it is highly likely that in the future, we might encounter a universal programming language. Think about it, by implementing AI, we no longer need to struggle with difficult or complex code. As AI advances, you will speak to computers in everyday language and they will execute tasks and operations accordingly.

One of the examples why a universal programming language is a possibility is Python. Python is one of the simplest programming languages you will ever come across. Programmers who exited the industry years back probably marvel at how easy things have become. It is widely expected that to build on this, it is possible to encounter a programming language that uses images and videos to interpret instructions and act on them.

More cloud computing

Let's bring this next innovation closer home with the example of a random Google search. Did you know that Google algorithms search through thousands of servers to deliver search results from a simple query? All this is to deliver the results you need in microseconds. Over the past decade, cloud computing has grown in leaps and bounds. However, this is not the end. There is still so much we can expect of cloud computing.

Many developers are still warming up to the prospect of working on the cloud. There are inherent concerns, especially the security of these cloud platforms, which still have a few developers skeptical about cloud computing. However, cloud computing is a reality.

It is easier to operate your applications on the cloud than having to maintain a server in your home. Local servers come with considerable risks. There is the risk of burglary, fire, power outage and so forth. All these are risks that might put you out of business. However, moving your work to the cloud means all these risks are taken over by the cloud service provider. All you have to do is upgrade your service packages as your needs scale up.

Concerns with Internet of Things (IoT)

We interact with so many IoT devices and concepts today. Quite a number of these devices are already in mainstream markets. Concerns about the security of these devices have risen in the past. Smart devices might make work easier, but they have so many loopholes that can be exploited and used against you. We can expect many cases of IoT security breaches in the near future, which will raise pertinent questions about the safety, data security and more importantly the role that the EU General Data Protection Regulation (GDPR) has to play in such scenarios as a watchdog in prudent data handling.

Chapter 9: Common Programming Challenges

The excitement about programming can fizzle out fast and turn into a nightmare. There are unexpected challenges that might make life difficult for you, especially as a beginner programmer. However, these challenges should not set you back or kill your resolve. They are common challenges that a lot of people have experienced before, and they overcame them, as you will too.

If you want to succeed in programming, you should be aware of the fact that mistakes do happen, and you will probably make many of them. The downside of mistakes is that you can feel you are not good enough. Everyone else seems to be doing fine, but not you. On the flip side, mistakes are an opportunity for you to learn and advance.

No one was born as good as they are today. What we are is the sum of mistakes and learning from those mistakes and experience. Feel free to reach out to mentors whenever you feel stuck. Deadlines and bug reports might overwhelm you, but once you get the hang of it, you will do great.

The following are some common challenges that you might experience as a beginner programmer.

Debugging

You feel content with a project, satisfied that it will run without a hitch and perform the desired duties. However, when you arrive at your desk in the morning, your quality assurance team has other ideas. They point out what seem like endless issues with the project. Perhaps the *OK* button is not responsive, the error messages are not displaying correctly and so forth.

All these are issues that eventually leave a negative impact on the user experience. You must get back to the drawing board and figure out where the problem lies. Debugging will be part of your life as a programmer. It is not enjoyable, but it is the reality.

Debugging is one of the most exhausting things you have to do. If you are lucky, you will encounter bugs that can be fixed easily. Most of the time, debugging costs you hours, and lots of coffee. However, do not feel downtrodden yet. Bugs are all over the place in programming. Even the best code you will ever come across needs debugging at some point.

Solution

How do you handle the debugging process and make your life easier? The first step is to document your work. Documentation might seem like a lot of work for you, but it helps you trace your steps in the event of an error. That way, you can easily trace the source and fix it, saving you from inspecting hundreds or thousands of code.

Another way of making light work of debugging is to recreate the problem. You must understand what the problem is before you try to solve it. If you recreate the problem, you isolate it from the rest of the code and get a better perspective of it.

Talk to someone. You might not always have all the answers. Do not fear anyone, especially if you work in a team. Beginner programmers often feel some people are out of reach, perhaps because of the positions they hold. However, if you do not ask for help, you will never really know whether the person will be helpful or not. The best person to ask for help, for example, is the quality tester who identified the problem, especially if you are unable to recreate the problem.

Working smart

As a programmer, one thing you must be aware of is that you will be sitting down for hours on end working on some code. This becomes your normal routine. You, however, are aware of the risks this poses to your health. Neck sprains, numb legs, back pain, pain in your palms and fingers from typing away all day. For a beginner, you might not be ready for the challenge yet. However, you must still dig in daily to meet your deliverables.

<u>Solution</u>

The first thing you must consider is regular exercise. If you work a desk job, it is possible to lose motivation and feel exhausted even before your workday is over. You can tackle this by keeping a workout routine. Jog before you go to work every morning, take a brisk half-hour walk and so forth. There are many simple routines that you can initiate which will help you handle the situation better.

While at work, take some time off and walk around–without looking like you are wasting time. This helps to relieve your body of the pain and pressure, and more importantly, allows for proper blood circulation. Other than that, you do not have to keep typing while seated. Stand up from time to time. Some companies have invested in height-adjustable desks, which help with this.

User experience

One of the most common challenges you will experience as a programmer is managing user experiences. You will come across a lot of clients in the course of your programming career. However, not all clients know how to communicate their needs. As a result, you will be involved in a lot of back and forth on project details and deliverables.

Most users have a good idea of what they need the project you are developing to do. However, this is not always the same as what your development team believes. Given that most beginner programmers never interact directly with the clients, especially in a team project, it might be difficult for you to understand them.

Solution

The best way around this is to figure out the best features of the project. Your client already knows what they want the project to do. Ask the right questions, especially to members of your team who are in direct contact with the client or the end user. The best responses will often come from designers and user experience experts. Their insight comes from interacting with users most of the time.

Another option is to test the product you are designing. You have probably used test versions of some products in the past. Most major players in the tech industry release beta versions of their products before the final. This way, users try it out, share their views, ideas and challenges they encounter. This information is collected and used to refine the beta product before the final one is released.

Testing your product allows you to identify and fix bugs before you release the product to the end user. It also allows you to interact with the user and gauge the level of acceptance for your project.

Estimates

A lot of beginner programmers struggle with scheduling. Perhaps you gave an estimate for a task and are unable to meet it. You are now a professional. Never delude yourself that you are not, perhaps because you are a beginner. This industry focuses on deadlines a lot. In software development, estimates are crucial. They are often used to plan bigger schedules for projects, and in some cases agree on the project quotes. Delays end up in problems that might in the long run affect trust between the parties involved.

Solution

The first step towards getting your estimates right is to apportion time properly. Time management is key. Set out a schedule within which you can complete a given task. Within that schedule, allow yourself ample buffer time for any inconvenience, but not too much time. For example, allow yourself 30-40 minutes for an assignment that should take 20 minutes.

Another way of improving your scheduling challenges is to break down assignments into micro milestones. A series of small tasks is easier to manage. Besides, when you complete these micro assignments, you are more psyched about getting onto the next one, and so on. You end up with a lighter workload which is also a good way to prevent burnout.

Constant updates

The tech industry keeps expanding in leaps and bounds. You can barely go a month before you learn about some groundbreaking work. Everything keeps upgrading or updating to better, more efficient versions. Libraries, tools and frameworks are not left behind either. Updates are awesome. Most updates improve user experiences, and bolster the platform security. However, updates come with undue pressure, even for the most experienced programmers out there.

Solution

Stay abreast with the latest developments in your field of expertise. You cannot know everything, but catching up on trends from time to time will help you learn some new tools and tips available, which can also help you improve on your skills and develop cutting edge products.

Another option is to learn. The beauty of the world of IT is that things are always changing. It is one of the most dynamic industries today. Carve out half an hour daily to learn something new. You will be intrigued by how much you will have mastered after a few weeks. In your spare time, challenge yourself to build something simple, solve a problem and so forth. There are lots of challenge websites available today where you can have a go at real-world problems.

Problems communicating

Beginner programmers face the communication challenge all the time. You are new to the workplace, so you do not really know anyone. Most of the team members and managers are alien to you, and as a result you often feel out of place. At some point in time every programmer goes through this. You feel like a baby among giants. Eventually, the pressure gets to you and you make a grave mistake, which could have been avoided if you reached out to someone to assist.

Solution

Dealing with communication problems is more than just a social interaction concern. First, you must learn to be proactive. If something bugs you, ask for help. The worst that can happen is people might laugh, especially if it is a rookie question, but someone will go out of their way and help you. If they don't and something goes awry, the department shoulders the blame for their ignorance. Before you know it, people will keep checking in on you to make sure you are getting it right, and you might also make some good friends in the process.

Consistency is another way to handle the communication challenge. For a beginner, you might not always get everything right. These are moments you can learn from. With practice, you grow bolder and learn to express yourself better over time.

Security concerns

Data is the new gold. This is the reality of the world right now. Data is precious, and is one of the reasons why tech giants are facing lawsuits all over the place. Huawei recently found themselves in a spat with the US government that ended up in a host of severed ties. There are so many reasons behind the hard stance that the US government took against Huawei, and most of them circle back to data.

People are willing to pay a great deal of money to access specific data that can benefit them in one way or the other. Some companies play the short-term game, others are in it for the long-term. Competitors also use nefarious ways to gain access to their competitors' databases and see what they are working on, and how they do it.

As a programmer, one thing your clients expect from you is that their data is safe, and the data their clients share with them through your project. Beginner programmers are fairly aware of all the security risks involved. This should not worry you so much, especially if you are part of a team of able developers. They will always have contingency measures in place. However, you must not be ignorant of security loopholes, especially in your code.

Solution

Hackers are always trying to gain access to some code. You cannot stop them from trying. You can, however, make it difficult for them to penetrate your code. Give them a challenge. The single biggest threat to any secure platform is human interaction. At times your code will not be compromised by someone from outside, but someone you know. In most cases, they compromise your code without knowing they do—unless they did it intentionally.

Make sure your workstation is safe. Every time you step away from your workstation, ensure your screen is locked, and if you are going away for a long time, shut down your devices.

In your programming language, it is also advisable that you use parameterized queries especially for SQL injections. This is important because most hackers use SQL injections to gain access and steal information.

Relying on foreign code

You have written some code for a few years and believe in your ability. You are confident you are good enough, hence being hired by the company. However, make peace with the fact that you will have to work on projects that were written by someone else. Working with another person's code is not always an easy thing, especially if their code seems outdated. There is a reason why the company insists on using that particular code.

The worst possible situation would be company politics–they occur everywhere. Someone wrote some code which the entire company relies on, but you cannot change or question it because the original coder has some connection with the company hierarchy. Often this raises a problem where you are unable to figure out the code.

<u>Solution</u>

Since there is not much you can do about the code, why not try to learn it? If you can, talk to the developer who wrote it and understand their reasoning behind it. This way, it is easier for you to embrace their style, and you will also have a smooth time handling your projects. You never know, you might just show them something new and help them rethink their code.

Another option is to embrace this code. It is not yours, but it is what you have and will be using for a very long time. Change your attitude about that code. Take responsibility for the code and work with it. This way, your hesitation will slowly fade away.

Lack of planning

While you have a burning desire to impress in your new place of work, you must have a plan. Many beginner programmers do not. Many programmers jump into writing code before stopping in their tracks to determine the direction they want to steer the code. The problem with this approach is that you will fail to make sense. The code might sound right in your head, but on paper nothing works.

<u>Solution</u>

Conceptualize an idea. Everything starts with an idea. Say you want to write a program that allows users to share important calendar dates and milestones with their loved ones. Focusing on this idea helps you remember why you are writing that code.

Once you have an idea, how do you connect it with real problems? What are the problems you are trying to solve? How are they connected to your idea? This also begs the question—why do people need your program?

Planning will help you save time when writing a program, and at the same time, help you stay on track.

Finally

In programming, everyone starts somewhere. Being the new person in the company should not scare you. Communicate with your peers and seniors, be willing to learn from them, and all the things that might seem overwhelming will somehow become easier as time goes by.

Conclusion

A career in computer programming is one of the most rewarding choices you will make in your life. However, brace yourself because it is not going to be an easy ride. Like any other career path, there is a learning curve that you must follow at your own pace. Do not be in a hurry to achieve greatness without laying your foundation first. Many people today are excited by the prospect of making it so fast that they ignore the important steps.

One of the reasons why you must be careful in the way you approach your career in computer programming is that without the right foundation, you will not cope with the advancements in the industry well. With a solid foundation, you can easily adapt because you are well-informed on the important languages and procedures necessary.

This book gives you a basic introduction to computer programming. Like most beginners, you might have been in a situation where you need to make a move, but are unsure of what lies ahead. The future in computer programming is diverse, and once you start, there is an endless list of possible outcomes for your future.

It is always easier to go with something that is close to your heart. Programming, as much as it is about skill and precision, is also about passion. If you are not passionate about the code you write, you will lose enthusiasm along the line. The slightest challenge in your path will have you rethinking your choices, which is not something you need to do.

As you begin this journey into programming, do not be cowed by the overshadowing tech giants around you. They too started from where you are. It took some of them longer to grasp some of the things you know today. Programmers tend to be a prideful bunch, so rest assured that some of them have barely mastered some skills, but cannot admit it.

In this incredible journey you will meet a lot of amazing people. Attend conferences, webinars and seminars whenever you can. These are enlightening moments that can change your perspective on many things. They are also a good place for you to interact with similar-minded folks and learn from them.

It is easy to think of yourself as a lone ranger when you start programming. However, this is not always true. You have a very good network of experts, tutors and friends online, some whom you will never meet, but who are committed to the greater good—a world where computer programming is a basic skill for everyone. Never be afraid to reach out and ask for help. Some of the best code you have interacted with was created by hard working teams that never gave up on each other.

It is not all milk and honey in computer programming. There will be risks and challenges too. In your career, you must also learn to figure out when you are in a dead-end environment. Some environments are unhealthy for budding programmers like yourself. Such an environment will stifle your growth and probably make you less enthusiastic about programming than you were when you started. My advice? Walk away from such an environment and mold your career elsewhere.

Remember that you are joining a world that is interconnected in more ways than you can imagine. Therefore, there is always the risk of security breaches, people stealing your code or injecting malicious code into yours, rendering it ineffective. People engage in all sorts of backhanded tactics to get the upper hand. This should not faze you. It is normal. There is always someone on the internet hoping they find a weakness they can exploit. Take the necessary precautions to shield your networks and devices from them.

Ultimately, computer programming is about solving problems in real-time and in the most efficient way. The world is never in short supply of problems. Programmers, therefore, are always working hard to fix something.

Think of yourself as one of the Avengers–Earth's Mightiest Heroes. This is your chance to change the world, one line of code at a time.

Good Luck!!

Made in the USA
Monee, IL
22 December 2020